CURTIS
& CHIP
A World of Possibility

Community Health Information
Partnership is supported by

Curtis Memorial Library

**Parkview Adventist
Medical Center**

Mid Coast Hospital

www.chiplibrary.org

HANDY HEALTH GUIDE TO YOUR EYES

**Alvin and Virginia Silverstein
and Laura Silverstein Nunn**

E Enslow Publishers, Inc.
40 Industrial Road
Box 398
Berkeley Heights, NJ 07922
USA

http://www.enslow.com

Original edition published as *Can You See the Chalkboard?* in 2001.

Library of Congress Cataloging-in-Publication Data

Silverstein, Alvin.
Handy health guide to your eyes / by Alvin Silverstein, Virginia Silverstein, and Laura Silverstein Nunn.
pages cm. — (Handy health guides)
  Summary: "Find out about the parts of the human eye and how we see, why things are blurry, if you need glasses or contacts, and how to take care of your eyes"—Provided by publisher.
Includes bibliographical references and index.
  ISBN 978-0-7660-4273-5
1. Eye—Care and hygiene—Juvenile literature. I. Silverstein, Virginia B. II. Nunn, Laura Silverstein. III. Title.
  RE51.S52 2014
  612.8'4—dc23
                              2012041455
Future editions:
Paperback ISBN: 978-1-4644-0489-4
EPUB ISBN: 978-1-4645-1253-7
Single-User PDF ISBN: 978-1-4646-1253-4
Multi-User PDF ISBN: 978-0-7660-5885-9

Printed in the United States of America
052013 Lake Book Manufacturing, Inc., Melrose Park, IL
10 9 8 7 6 5 4 3 2 1

To Our Readers: We have done our best to make sure all Internet Addresses in this book were active and appropriate when we went to press. However, the author and the publisher have no control over and assume no liability for the material available on those Internet sites or on other Web sites they may link to. Any comments or suggestions can be sent by e-mail to comments@enslow.com or to the address on the back cover.

Illustration Credits: Carolyn A. McKeone/Photo Researchers, Inc., p. 25; David Parker/Photo Researchers, Inc., p. 34 (right); Iakov Filimonov/Photos.com, p. 6; @ iStockphoto.com/drbimages (girl), p. 1; @ iStockphoto.com/ Michael Henderson, p. 20; Jaimie Duplass/Photos.com, p. 39; Jose antonio Sanchez reyes/Photos.com, p. 19; Jupiterimages/Photos.com, p. 8; Juraj Lenhard/Photos.com, p. 28; mocker_bat/Photos.com, p. 1 (girl); Ralph C. Eagle, Jr./Photo Researchers, Inc./Colorization by: Robin Treadwell, p. 12; Shutterstock.com, pp. 1 (glasses, etc.), 3, 4, 7, 9, 10, 13, 14, 15, 16, 17, 21, 22, 24, 26, 29, 30, 32, 33, 34 (left), 35, 38, 40, 41.

Cover Photo: mocker_bat/Photos.com (girl); iStockphoto.com/Thinkstock (accessories)

CONTENTS

Can you see the whiteboard in your classroom? If not, tell an adult. You may need to see an eye doctor.

1

WHEN THINGS LOOK BLURRY

Do you have trouble seeing the chalkboard clearly in school? Do things look blurry when you look at a computer screen or a video game? Do you rub your eyes and squint a lot? These are all signs that your eyes aren't working quite right.

Your eyes are remarkable. You use them to see a rainbow of colors and a variety of shapes. You can see in bright sunshine or almost total darkness.

Your eyes let you see where you are going. They help you look out for cars before crossing the street. They keep you from bumping into furniture or tripping over things on the floor. Most importantly, your eyes also help you learn about and understand the world.

If you can see objects clearly from both far away and close up, you have good vision. But if some things look blurry to you, you probably have poor vision. Don't worry, though—an opthalmologist, or eye doctor, can test your eyes to find out what's wrong. You may need eyeglasses to help you see better. But if you don't want

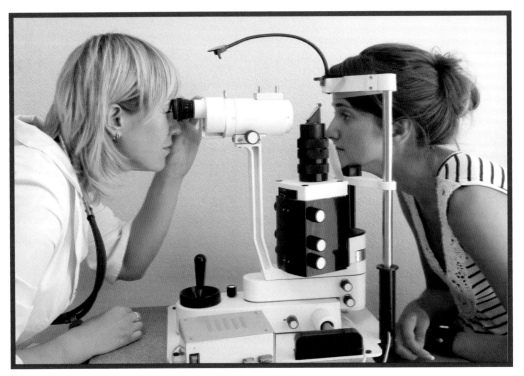

An eye doctor does a series of tests to check your vision and the health of your eyes. One of these exams is done with a slit lamp, a microscope with a light attached. It lets the doctor closely examine your cornea, iris, and lens.

to wear glasses, you may be able to wear contact lenses instead.

Whether you have perfect vision or wear glasses, there are some things you can do to keep your eyes healthy and strong. Read on to learn more about how your eyes work and what you can do if something goes wrong.

Handy Healthy Fact

Your Eyes Are the Windows to the World

Your eyes are your most important sense organ. About 80 percent of the information you gather about the world comes through your eyes.

2

INSIDE YOUR EYES

When you look at yourself in the mirror, you can see only a small part of your eyes. But there's more to your eyes than what you can see. What you're looking at is just the front part of your eyeball. An eyeball looks a bit like a big round marble. But a marble is hard, whereas an eyeball is soft. An eyeball is filled with a jellylike liquid.

Your eyelids protect your eyes. You can move them up and down like window shades. You can close them if the light is

The eyeball is round like a marble, but you see only the front part of it.

Blink Away

You may not realize it, but your eyes blink all the time. Unless your eyes are closed, you blink between six and thirty times each minute.

too bright. If an insect or a bit of dust zooms in toward your eyes, your eyelids quickly snap shut—you blink. Blinking is automatic. You don't even have to think about it.

Blinking allows your eyelid to work like a pump. The closing action squeezes out a bit of liquid from your tear gland and then spreads it evenly over your cornea—the clear covering on the surface of the eye. You make tears all the time. This keeps the eyes moist so the corneas won't dry out and get sore.

If you look at someone's eyes, you could look right through the cornea and see the iris—the colored part of the eye. The color of a person's iris depends on the amount of pigment in it. Brown eyes have a lot of pigment; blue eyes have less.

9

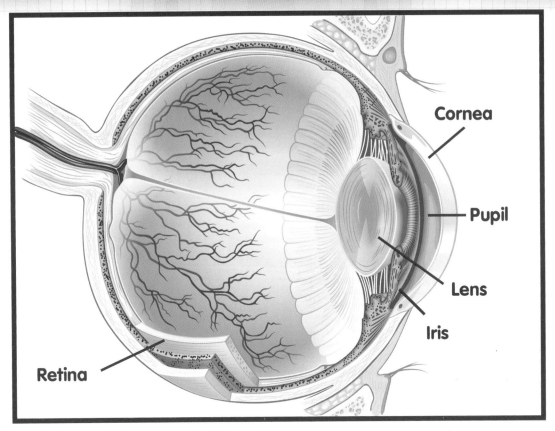

Cornea

Pupil

Lens

Iris

Retina

This drawing of the eye shows some parts you can't see in the mirror.

The black dot in the middle of your iris is an opening called the pupil. Light rays enter your eye through the pupil. Muscles inside the iris can change the size of your pupil. When you are in a dark place, your pupils get larger so more light can enter your eyes. When you are in a bright place, your pupil gets smaller to let in less light.

Activity 1: How Big Are Your Pupils?

To see how light affects the size of your pupils, stand in front of a mirror in a sunny room. Look closely at your pupils. Now cover your eyes with your hands for about ten seconds. While your eyes are blocked from the light, your pupils will get larger. Uncover your eyes and look at them in the mirror. You should see your pupils getting smaller and smaller as they adjust to the amount of light in the room.

Next, shine a flashlight near one eye. The sudden bright light makes your pupil get smaller. What happens to the pupil in your other eye? It should get smaller, too, because the pupils work together. Like blinking, these reactions are automatic. You cannot control them.

Scientists have found that people's pupils also get larger when they are looking at something interesting, and they get smaller when they see something upsetting. Show your friends some pictures in a magazine. Write down what happens to their pupils when they see each picture. Do their pupils get bigger when they look at a laughing baby? Do their pupils get smaller when they see a war scene?

Behind the pupil is a clear structure called the lens. Light rays pass through the lens and travel through the fluid in the eyeball. Then they strike the retina, a layer of light-sensitive cells that lines the back of the eyeball. Here, they form a picture, called an image.

Two kinds of cells in the retina respond to light. These cells are named for their shapes: rods and cones. Rod cells are shaped like short, straight sticks. Cone cells look similar to upside down ice cream cones. We need both rods and cones for good vision.

The rod cells in your retina can pick up tiny bits of light. They help you see shapes and movement in dim light, but the vision they provide is blurry and unclear. Cone cells are sensitive only to bright light. There are three different kinds of cone cells. Each cone cell reacts to just one kind of light—red, green, or blue. When you look at a green shirt, your green cone cells react, but the red and blue cells do not.

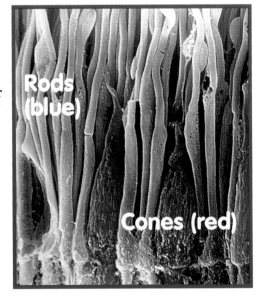

This magnified view of the retina shows rods and cones, which are artificially colored.

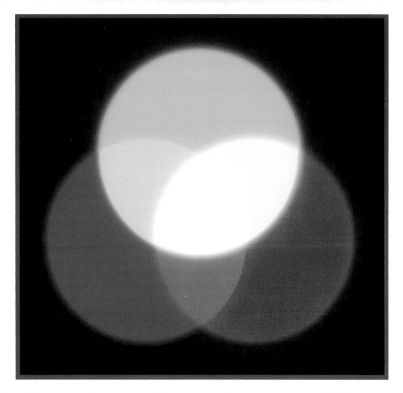

The three primary colors—red, green, and blue—can be combined to make many different colors.

If there are just three kinds of cones, you might wonder how you see other colors. Your cone cells can work together. For example, when both your red and blue cones react, you see purple. Red, green, and blue are called primary colors because every other color can be made by combining them. Your cone cells thus allow you to see all the colors of the rainbow.

When you go outside on a moonlit evening, there is not enough light for your cone cells to work. Only the rod cells can react. That's why you can't see colors at night. You can still make out shapes, but things are all in shades of gray.

All of the cone cells are located in the fovea, a small area of the retina directly behind the lens. The image formed on the fovea is much clearer and more detailed than the image projected onto the rest of the retina, where there are only rods.

Handy Healthy Fact

Eagle Eyes

There are about 160,000 cone cells per square millimeter in the fovea of a human eye. That may seem like a lot, but an eagle's fovea has about 1 million cone cells per square millimeter! That is why an eagle's vision is about six times as sharp as ours—sharp enough to spot a mouse scurrying through the grass far below.

3

HOW YOUR EYES SEE

What do you see when you are reading a book? You might say you are looking at a bunch of pages with words on them. What you are really seeing is light. When you look at an object, such as a book, light is reflected—or mirrored—back to your eyes.

You cannot see without light. When light rays hit your eyes, they pass through the cornea. The cornea bends the light so it enters the lens. The lens bends the light rays even more.

The words you read on a page are actually reflected light.

As the light rays make their way through the liquid inside the eyeball, they continue to bend. All this bending makes the light rays from each point of the object you are looking at fall onto a single point on the retina. This process is called focusing. Together, all these focused points form an image—a picture of the object.

Because of the way the light rays are bent, the image that forms on the retina is upside down. This image is turned into nerve signals, which are then sent to the brain along a thick cord of nerve cells that form the optic nerve. Special areas of the brain receive and

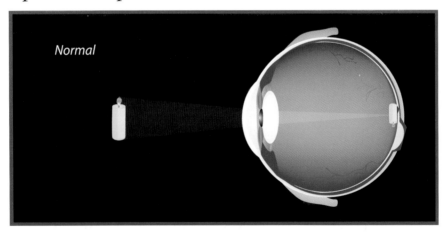

Normal

When you look at something, all the light rays from each point on the object are bent so that they fall onto a single point on the retina and form an image.

interpret the messages from the eyes. You don't really "see" anything until your brain makes sense out of the message from the eyes and turns the image right side up.

If you are reading a book and you hear a friend call your name, you may look up to see what is going on. When you do this, your eyes need to quickly make some changes to focus on your friend's face. To see a more distant object, muscles in your eyes will pull on your lenses to make them flatter. When you look back at the book, the muscles relax and your lenses form a more curved shape. Every time you look at something new, your eyes must refocus.

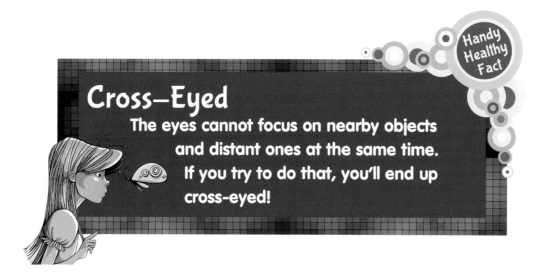

Cross-Eyed
The eyes cannot focus on nearby objects and distant ones at the same time. If you try to do that, you'll end up cross-eyed!

Activity 2: Seeing in 3–D

Close one eye and try to walk around the room. Did you have trouble? Did you bump into anything? Walking around with one eye closed is not impossible, but it's much easier to walk when you have both your eyes open. That's because seeing through just one eye gives you only part of the picture. The image looks flat and two-dimensional.

When you look at an object with both eyes open, each eye sees an image at a slightly different angle. When your brain combines these images, you get a three-dimensional view. Seeing in 3-D helps you understand how far away you are from the object. It helps you catch a ball and avoid bumping into things.

4

WHAT'S WRONG WITH THIS PICTURE?

Most of the time, we see the world in clear, colorful, three-dimensional images. But sometimes eyes don't work properly. For some people, the pictures don't look right—they appear strange and unclear.

Sometimes your eyes need to take a rest. When you use your eyes too much for one task, the muscles may get tired and you may get blurry vision. If your eyes feel tired or achy and you have a headache, you probably have eyestrain. When this happens, pay attention to your eyes—take a break!

Your eyes may get overworked and tired if you use them too much.

Morning Eyes

Did you ever have blurry vision when you first open your eyes in the morning? But then after a while, things look clear again? While you sleep at night, fluid builds up in the corneas. This causes swelling that changes the way they bend light rays. It takes a little while for the corneas to get back to normal. So your vision will be clearer at midmorning than when you first wake up.

Blurry vision may also be a sign of a more serious problem. If you can see close objects fairly well, but have trouble seeing things that are far away, you may have myopia. Myopia is also called nearsightedness because you can clearly see only objects that are nearby. If you are nearsighted, your eyeball is a little longer (from front to back) than normal. Light rays from distant objects meet before they reach your retina. By the time the light rays strike the retina, they have spread out and form a blurred image.

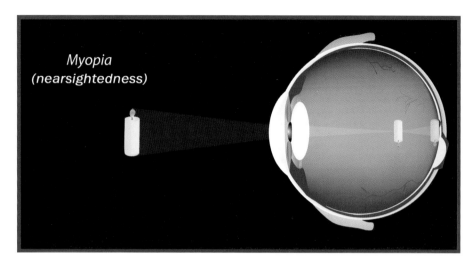

Myopia
(nearsightedness)

If you are nearsighted, nearby objects may look clear, but distant objects are blurry because your eyeball is so long that the rays of light come together before they reach your retina.

There is no way to clear up the distant image because the lens can't adjust the focusing well enough to get the light rays to come together on the retina. Squinting helps a bit. Fewer light rays come in through the narrowed opening, so they haven't spread out as much by the time they reach the retina.

Nearsightedness usually shows up in young school-age kids. Nearsighted children often have trouble seeing the chalkboard clearly if they are sitting in the back of the classroom.

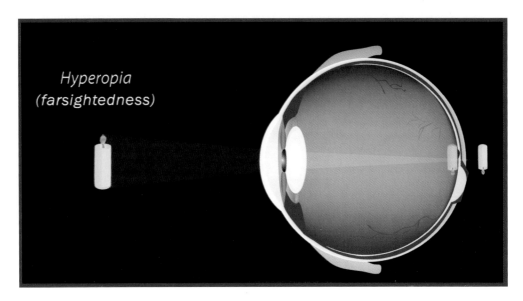

*Hyperopia
(farsightedness)*

If you are farsighted, you can see distant objects clearly, but nearby things are blurry because your eyeball is too short for the light rays to come together on your retina.

If you have no trouble seeing objects that are far away, but things that are close to you look blurry, you may have hyperopia. Hyperopia is also called farsightedness because you can clearly see only objects that are far away. If you are farsighted, your eyeball is a little shorter than normal. Light rays from close objects reach the retina before they can meet, causing a blurred image.

Normally, muscles in the eye make the lens rounder and thicker to bring close objects into focus. If you are farsighted, your muscles cannot make your lens round and thick enough to bring light rays into focus on the retina. You can see distant objects because light rays from faraway things come in nearly straight, so it is possible to focus them. However, because your eye muscles work very hard, you may experience eyestrain and headaches.

If everything looks a little blurry to you, you may have a different condition called astigmatism. This means your cornea is not shaped quite right. Your cornea is supposed to be perfectly round, like a basketball. But the cornea of a person with astigmatism may be shaped more like a football. The cornea may also bulge out a little in some places or dip in at others. When this happens, light rays cannot come together at a single point on the retina.

To make things even more complicated, some people with astigmatism may also be either nearsighted or farsighted. There are many different things that can affect your vision. That's why it's a good idea to have a doctor take a look at your eyes.

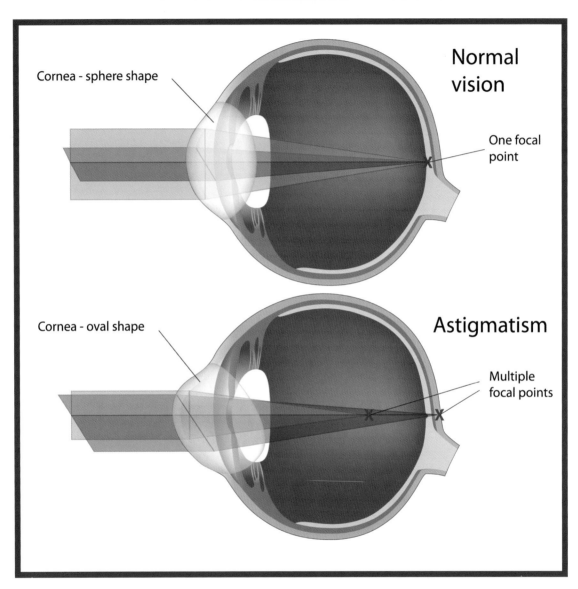

Normal vision

Cornea - sphere shape

One focal point

Cornea - oval shape

Astigmatism

Multiple focal points

In astigmatism, the abnormal shape of the eyes makes things both close and far away appear blurry because light rays are focused at different points on the retina.

This child has lazy eye.

Some people do not see well because their eyes have trouble working together. Most of the time, muscles on the outside of a person's eyes turn the eyeballs inward to look at a close object. In some people, one eyeball turns too much in one direction—either toward the nose or toward the side. As a result, each eye sees a different picture and sends a very different message to the brain. One image is clear and sharp, but the other is blurry. This may cause double vision—seeing two images at the same time.

Eventually, the brain may learn to "turn off" the blurry view. But using only one eye gives a flat, two-dimensional view, instead of a three-dimensional picture. This condition is known as amblyopia, or lazy eye. Lazy eye usually appears in very young children. If it is not caught early enough, the unused eye may lose its ability to see.

Do you have trouble telling the difference between colors? If you do, you may be color-blind. Color-blind people are born with missing cone cells. If you are red-green color-blind, you are missing either red or green cones. As a result, red and green look like the same color. Color blindness is more common in males than females. There is no treatment. People just learn to live with the condition.

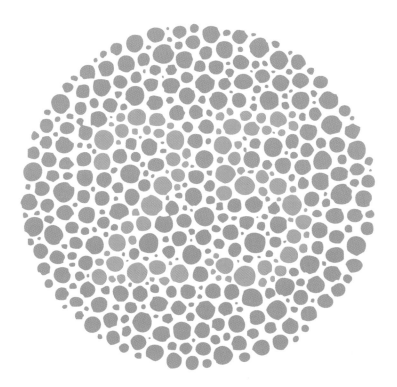

Can you see the number 25? If not, you may be color-blind.

5

DO YOU NEED GLASSES?

How do you know if you have a vision problem? You may be so used to seeing the world a certain way that you don't realize that anything is wrong. If things have looked blurry all your life, how could you know what clear images are supposed to look like?

Vision screening tests in schools can catch many eye problems early, but the best way to find out is to see an eye doctor. The doctor will test your eyes to make sure they are healthy and working properly.

First the eye doctor will ask you a couple of basic questions. For example, do things appear blurry to you? Or, does anyone in your family wear glasses or have any eye problems? Then the doctor will ask you to read

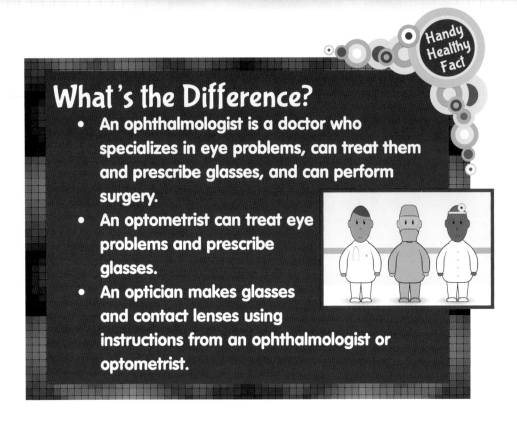

What's the Difference?

- An ophthalmologist is a doctor who specializes in eye problems, can treat them and prescribe glasses, and can perform surgery.
- An optometrist can treat eye problems and prescribe glasses.
- An optician makes glasses and contact lenses using instructions from an ophthalmologist or optometrist.

from an eye chart. The doctor uses this eye chart to find out how well you can see.

The doctor may also do other tests to check for nearsightedness, farsightedness, and astigmatism. After studying the test results, the doctor will know whether you need eyeglasses.

The lenses in eyeglasses work like the lenses in your eyes. They are carefully made to bend light rays in a way that will make images focus properly on your retina.

E

E P

T O Z

L P E D

P E C F D

E D F C Z P

F E L O P Z D
D E F P O T E C

L E F O D P C T
F D P L N C E O

A doctor may use an eye chart like this one to test a person's vision.

No two people have exactly the same eye problem, so no two people have exactly the same eyeglasses.

Nearsightedness is corrected with lenses that are thin in the middle and thick at the edges. When light rays pass through these lenses, they are bent outward just enough so that they come together at the retina.

Farsightedness is corrected with lenses that are thick in the middle and thin at the edges. When light rays pass through these lenses, they are bent inward enough to meet at the retina and form a clear image.

If you have astigmatism, light rays do not strike a single point on your retina. That can be solved with eyeglasses that add a different curve at the irregular parts of your eye. As a result, light rays bend just the right amount and focus on your retina.

This ophthalmologist is using a machine to determine exactly what kind of eyeglass lenses will correct this person's vision.

Do You Have 20/20 Vision?

Have you ever heard people talk about having 20/20 eyesight? What does that mean? 20/20 means that you can read the letters from an eye chart that people with normal vision can see at twenty feet. If the doctor says that you have a score of 20/30 that means that you were able to read a line at 20 feet away that people with normal vision could make out at 30 feet. So your vision is not as sharp as people with normal vision. Each eye is tested separately. You can score differently in each eye.

Some children with lazy eye wear glasses. Others may wear a patch. When their good eye is covered, they have no choice but to use their weak eye. Special eye exercises can also help make the weak eye stronger. There is a much better chance of correcting lazy eye if it is treated early.

You may feel strange when you wear glasses for the first time. Objects may look a little blurry or unclear. This is perfectly normal. It may take several days for your brain to get used to what objects are supposed to look like.

6

ARE CONTACTS FOR YOU?

Have you ever gotten an eyelash or a speck of dirt in your eye? Did it bother you so much that your eye got red and watery? If so, you might wonder how people can put contact lenses in their eyes.

Although your eyes are very sensitive to small objects, such as a tiny eyelash, large objects that follow the curve of the eyeball don't bother them. Otherwise, the feeling of your own eyelids would drive you crazy!

A contact lens is a very thin plastic disk that can be placed

With practice, you can learn to insert a contact lens correctly.

on the front surface of your eye. It is separated from the cornea by a thin film of tears, which holds the lens in place. Like glasses, contact lenses are designed to correct vision problems. Millions of people wear contact lenses, but they are not right for everybody.

Before you get contacts, you should ask yourself a few questions. Will you have trouble putting something in your eyes? You need to keep contacts clean and germ-free. Are you willing to spend time doing that?

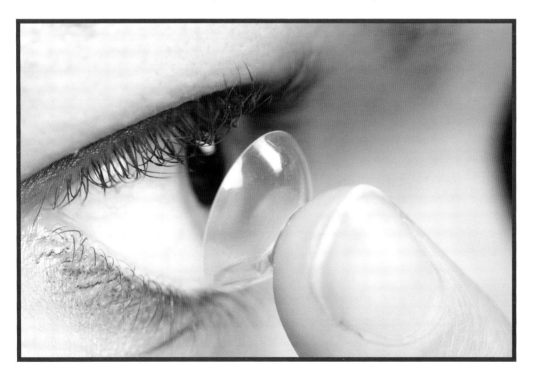

A contact lens fits snugly over the curve of your eyeball. It floats on a thin film of tears.

People often choose to wear contacts because they think they look better without glasses. But that's not the only reason to wear contacts. They may actually be more helpful for certain eye problems, such as nearsightedness. When a nearsighted person looks through glasses, objects straight ahead appear clear but objects to the right or left may look blurry. Because contacts rest on top of the eyeball and move with the eyes, the person sees everything clearly.

Contacts come in hard and soft lenses. Soft contact lenses are very popular because they are flexible and feel more comfortable than hard contacts. Soft contacts

 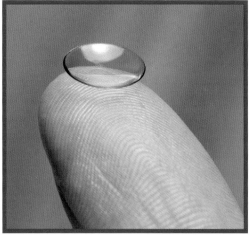

A soft contact lens (left) is flexible and can mold to the eye's curved shape. A hard contact lens (right) keeps a rigid shape—it doesn't bend.

Colored Contacts
Tinted contact lenses can make your iris look like it is a different color.

mold to the eye's shape and feel more natural. However, hard lenses provide sharper vision and are less likely to tear than soft contacts. Another problem with soft lenses is that they often soak up liquids, such as tears, and may pick up bacteria and particles that can irritate your eyes. As a result, there is a greater risk of the eyes becoming infected with soft lenses.

Many people take out their contacts every night and clean them with a special eye-care solution. Disposable contacts—available in both hard and soft lenses—can be worn for up to two weeks and then thrown away. Doctors say that even disposable contacts should be cleaned every day, however.

If you'd like to wear contacts, but don't want to deal with cleaning them, there are actually one-day disposables. You wear them for one day and then throw them away. These lenses provide clear vision and keep the eyes healthy and free from particles. So they are actually very healthy for your eyes.

Before you decide whether you want glasses or contact lenses, you need to talk to your eye doctor. If contacts are for you, a complete eye exam will help the doctor fit you with the right ones.

7
TAKE CARE OF YOUR EYES

Whether or not you wear glasses, it is important to take care of your eyes. Fortunately, there are many things you can do to keep your eyes healthy and strong.

Have you ever read a book or played on the computer for a really long time? Your eyes probably started to hurt. Maybe the images even got a little fuzzy? That's because your eye muscles were being overworked.

If you use your eyes for a long time, take several breaks and give them a rest. If you've been focusing on something close, stare out a window or look at a peaceful picture on the wall for a few minutes. You could also try closing your eyes and covering them with your hands for a little while. You might even want to lie down or lean back in a comfortable chair.

Don't use a computer in the dark. Turning on a light can cut down on the eye-tiring glare of the screen.

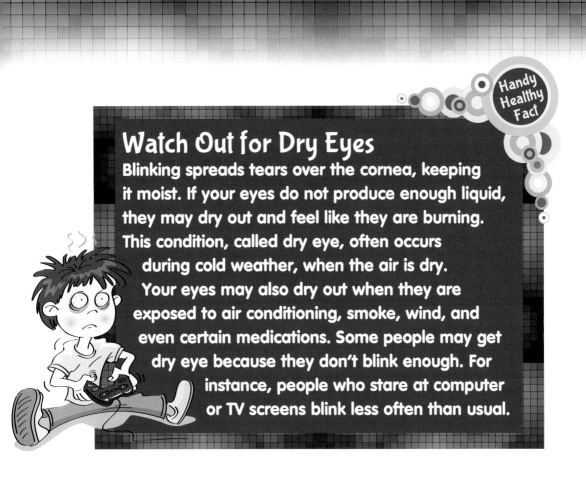

Watch Out for Dry Eyes

Blinking spreads tears over the cornea, keeping it moist. If your eyes do not produce enough liquid, they may dry out and feel like they are burning. This condition, called dry eye, often occurs during cold weather, when the air is dry. Your eyes may also dry out when they are exposed to air conditioning, smoke, wind, and even certain medications. Some people may get dry eye because they don't blink enough. For instance, people who stare at computer or TV screens blink less often than usual.

The glare from a computer or TV screen can also make your eyes hurt. A glare causes your eyes to work harder to focus on the picture. Reducing the glare will make the picture appear clearer, so there's less work for your eyes.

Also, always keep at least one light on while you watch TV. A darkened room means that your eyes have to strain to focus to get a clear view. Your eyes shouldn't have to work so hard.

Wearing sunglasses can protect your eyes and make you look cool at the same time.

Too much sunlight can also damage your eyes. Never look directly at the sun. Most sunglasses sold today are specially designed to block out some of the sun's dangerous rays.

For a healthy body, doctors say you should eat healthy foods. That goes for your eyes too. Carrots, milk, cheese, eggs, broccoli, spinach, sweet potato, cantaloupe, and other foods rich in vitamin A are important in keeping your eyes healthy.

If you look out for your eyes now, chances are you will have a much clearer, brighter future.

Handy Healthy Fact

Eye Muscles
You move your eye muscles at least 100,000 times a day.

GLOSSARY

amblyopia (am-blee-OH-pee-uh)—A condition that occurs when a person's eyes do not work together properly, also called lazy eye.

astigmatism (uh-STIG-muh-tihz-um)—A condition in which an irregular shape of the cornea prevents clear focusing of images.

color-blind—Being unable to tell the difference between some or all the colors that most people see.

cone cells—Light-sensitive cells that respond only to bright light and provide for color vision.

contact lens—A plastic disk that is placed over the cornea and helps a person see.

cornea—The clear covering on the surface of the eye.

double vision—Seeing two images at the same time.

dry eye—A condition in which the eye does not produce enough tears, causing dry, hot, burning eyes.

eyeball—The round, jelly-filled structure that contains all the working parts of the eye.

eyelid—A movable flap of skin over the eye that protects the eye from dust and particles.

eyestrain—Blurred images, tired eyes, or headaches caused by overworking the eyes.

focusing—Bending of the light rays from each point on an object so that they fall onto a single point on the retina and form an image.

fovea—A small area of the retina directly behind the lens. It contains all the cones and produces a clear, colorful image.

hyperopia (hy-pur-OH-pee-uh)—A condition in which distant objects appear clear, but close objects are blurry; also called farsightedness.

image—The appearance of an object.

iris—The colored part of the eye. It contains muscles that change the size of the pupil to control the amount of light coming in.

lens—A clear structure behind the pupil that bends light rays to focus them on the retina.

myopia (my-OH-pee-uh)—A condition in which close objects appear clear, but distant objects are blurry; also called nearsightedness.

ophthalmologist (ahp-thuhl-MAHL-uh-jist)—A doctor who specializes in eye problems, can prescribe glasses, and can perform surgery on people's eyes.

optic nerve—A thick cord of nerve cells that carries messages from the eyes to the brain.

optician (ahp-TIH-shun)—Someone who makes glasses and contact lenses using instructions from an ophthalmologist or optometrist.

optometrist (ahp-TOM-uh-trihst)—Someone who tests people's eyesight and makes and sells glasses.

pigment—A colored chemical.

primary colors—Red, blue, and green, the three colors used to create all other colors.

pupil—The opening in the eye that allows light rays to travel to the retina.

reflection—Bouncing of light rays from an object back to the eyes.

retina—A layer of light-sensitive cells that lines the back of the eyeball.

rod cells—Light-sensitive cells that respond to dim light, providing night vision.

tear gland—A tiny structure next to the eyeball that produces tears.

vision—Eyesight.

FURTHER READING

Books

Ballard, Carol. *Why Do I Need Glasses?* Chicago: Raintree, 2011.

Morgan, Philip. *Sensing the World*. Mankato, Minn.: Amicus, 2012.

Stewart, Melissa. *The Eyes Have It: The Secrets of Eyes and Seeing*. Pelham, N.Y.: Benchmark Books, 2009.

Walker, Richard, John Woodward and Ben Morgan. *Human Body: A Visual Encyclopedia*. New York: DK Publishing, 2012.

Web Sites

KidsHealth. "Your Eyes."
   <http://kidshealth.org/kid/htbw/eyes.html>

The National Eye Institute. "See All You Can See: Parts
   of the Eye." <isee.nei.nih.gov/parts>

INDEX